A ROOKIE BIOGRAPHY

THURGOOD MARSHALL

First African-American Supreme Court Justice

By Carol Greene

CHILDRENS PRESS ®

CHICAGO

This book is for John Russell.

Thurgood Marshall

Library of Congress Cataloging-in-Publication Data

Greene, Carol.
    Thurgood Marshall : (first African American Supreme Court Justice) /
by Carol Greene.
        p.   cm. — (A Rookie biography)
    Summary: A biography of the first African American to be appointed
to the Supreme Court.
    ISBN 0-516-04225-4
    1. Marshall, Thurgood, 1908-1993—Juvenile literature. 2. Afro-
American judges—Biography—Juvenile literature. [1. Marshall,
Thurgood, 1908-1993 2. Afro-Americans—Biography. 3. United States.
Supreme Court—Biography.] I. Title. II. Series: Greene, Carol. Rookie
biography.
KF8745.M34G74   1991
347.73′2634—dc20
[B]
[347.3073534]
[B]   91-4798
                                                                    CIP
                                                                     AC

Thurgood Marshall
is a real person.
As a lawyer, he
fought for the rights
of African Americans.
As a justice
on the Supreme Court,
he fought for the rights
of all Americans.
This is his story.

TABLE OF CONTENTS

Slaves captured in Africa were brought
to America to work for their owners.
Slaves were treated as property—
they were bought and sold like houses
or horses. Slaves were not free.

Chapter 1

A Family of Fighters

Thurgood came from
a family of fighters.
He liked to hear
stories about them.

There was great-grandfather,
a slave, brought
to America from
"the toughest part of the Congo."

Great-grandfather was
so full of fight that
his owner set him free
and asked him to go away.

Grandfather Marshall wanted
to fight in the Union army
during the Civil War.
But he didn't have a first name
and he couldn't join
the army without one.

This drawing was used on a poster asking African Americans to join the Union army. The black soldiers were led by white officers.

Above: Company E, 4th U.S. Colored Infantry at Fort Lincoln in 1865. Thousands of black soldiers, like the unknown soldier at left, fought bravely for the Union in the Civil War.

So Grandfather Marshall
made up his own name
—Thorough Good.
Thurgood was named for him.

Thurgood's father, Will,
liked to fight with words.
He and his sons,
Thurgood and Aubrey,
would sit in their home
in Baltimore, Maryland,
and argue about almost
anything—even the weather.

Baltimore is
famous for
its row houses
with marble
front steps.

Will wanted his sons
to learn to think straight.
He wanted them
to be strong, too.

Once he told Thurgood,
"Son, if anyone ever
calls you a nigger,
you not only got my
permission to fight him
—you got my orders
to fight him."

Thurgood had his first fight
when he was 10.
He thought his brother
had turned over a wagon
full of food.
So he yelled at him.

Aubrey was 13 then.
Thurgood lost that fight.

When Thurgood was 13,
a white man grabbed him,
made him drop some boxes,
and called him "nigger."

Thurgood punched him.
Then he punched him again.
At last, a policeman
broke up the fight.

Thurgood could have been
in a lot of trouble.
But the policeman knew him,
and another man had seen
what really happened.

His parents were proud of him.
Thurgood knew that.
But his mother worried, too.
She didn't want Thurgood
to be mean.

Norma Marshall wanted
Thurgood to be a dentist
when he grew up.
That took studying, though,
and Thurgood didn't like
studying very much.

Chapter 2

Changes

When Thurgood got
in trouble at school,
he had to go to the
school basement
and learn parts of
the United States
Constitution
by heart. He
learned many parts.

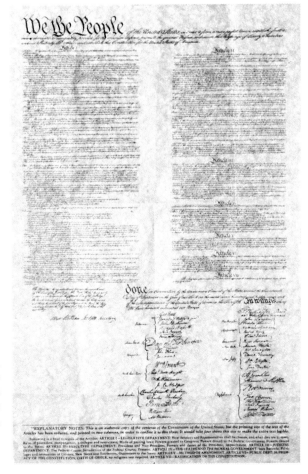

The United States Constitution
grants certain rights to the
people. Marshall was to argue
that these rights belong to *all* the
people—not just to white people.

But in high school,
Thurgood changed.
He made good grades.
Then he went on
to Lincoln University
in Pennsylvania.

Students at Lincoln University in Pennsylvania walk under
the Memorial Arch at the entrance to the campus.

Future medical doctors study anatomy at Lincoln University.

There he began studying
to be a dentist.
But he joined
the debating team too.

Thanks to his father,
Thurgood was good
at fighting with words.
He worked harder at
debating than at anything else.

At last he decided he
should not be a dentist.
He should be a lawyer.
Lawyers help people
by fighting with words.
He'd be a good lawyer.

Thurgood also fell in love.
The girl's name was Vivien,
but he called her Buster.
They didn't have much money,
but they got married anyway
and were very happy.

Thurgood wanted to go
to law school at the
University of Maryland.
But the school wouldn't
let him come there
because he was black.

So he went to law school
at Howard University
in Washington, D.C.

The library building at Howard
University in Washington, D.C.

There Thurgood graduated
at the top of his class.
He went back to Baltimore
and worked for the NAACP—the
National Association for the
Advancement of Colored People.

Thurgood Marshall (right) worked with another lawyer, U. Simpson Tate,
to stop the state of Texas from closing NAACP offices.

Thurgood Marshall (fourth from left) photographed with other lawyers working for the NAACP Legal Defense and Educational Fund, Inc.

Both blacks and whites
belonged to the NAACP.
They worked for fair treatment
of African Americans.

Ten years after Marshall helped Donald Murray (left) enter the University of
Maryland law school, Murray helped Heman Sweatt (right). Sweatt was going
to court because he wanted to enter the University of Texas law school.

One day, Donald Murray,
a young black man,
came to see Thurgood.
He wanted to go
to law school at the
University of Maryland.

Would Thurgood help him?
Thurgood couldn't wait to start!

He worked hard on Murray's case.
He read and he thought.
He remembered those parts
of the U.S. Constitution
he'd learned long ago.
Now he would use them.

At the trial, Thurgood said
it was Murray's *right*
to go to that law school.
The Constitution said so.

When the trial was over,
Thurgood had won.
He went outside the court
and danced for joy.

Segregation in America meant separate public facilities for whites and blacks as well as separate schools. The Supreme Court had ruled in 1896 that such "separate but equal" accommodations were constitutional. Thurgood Marshall said they were unconstitutional.

WHITE PASSENGERS
Please Fill Seats From Front of Car
COLORED PASSENGERS
From Rear

Chapter 3

A Victory for Children

Again and again, Thurgood
fought for African Americans
who were treated unfairly.
Many were poor, so he
didn't earn much money.
He didn't care about that.

In 1936, he went to work for
the NAACP in New York City.
He still didn't earn much.
But he fought some
very important battles.

Many people objected to school desegregation. Whites
protested when Elizabeth Echford (left) entered Central High School
in Little Rock, Arkansas, and when black children
entered an elementary school in New Orleans (right).

In those days, many states
made black children
and white children go
to different schools.
This is called segregation.

Thurgood fought segregation
wherever he could.
In the early 1950s,
he fought his biggest battle.

Linda Brown was
a black girl
in Topeka, Kansas.
She had to go
to a school for
black children.

Nine-year-old Linda Brown photographed in 1952

Linda's father was a minister.
He thought all children
should go to school together.
So he sued the Topeka
Board of Education.

Thurgood Marshall stands in front of the Supreme Court building.

The case went from court
to court, until it got to
the Supreme Court, the
highest court in the United States.
Thurgood was the lawyer
for Linda's father.

He told the Supreme Court
that segregation was
against the Constitution.
He said black children should
be equal to white children.

One justice asked what
Thurgood meant by "equal."

"Equal," said Thurgood, "means
getting the *same* thing,
at the *same* time,
and in the *same* place."

A mother explains the importance of the Supreme Court decision to her daughter.

It took the Supreme Court
a long time to decide.
But on May 17, 1954,
the justices said segregation
was against the Constitution.

They also said segregation
hurt the hearts and minds
of black children
—sometimes forever.
From now on, blacks and whites
must go to school together.

Thurgood had won
his greatest victory,
a victory for children.

The winning lawyers (left to right: George E. C. Hayes, Thurgood Marshall,
James M. Nabrit) leave the Supreme Court building after the historic
Brown v. Board of Education decision outlawed segregation in public schools.

Cecilia Marshall

Chapter 4

Important Jobs

Early in 1955,
Thurgood's wife, Buster,
died of cancer.
Thurgood missed her
so much that he worked
almost all the time.

Then he found
a new wife, Cecilia.
They had two boys.

Thurgood and Cecilia Marshall with their sons Thurgood, Jr. (right), and John.

Thurgood loved to play with
Thurgood, Junior, and John.
He taught them to
think straight, the way
his father had taught him.

Marshall is surrounded by books in his New York home.

By this time, many people
could see that Thurgood
was a fine lawyer
and a good man.
He began to get
some very important jobs.

On September 23, 1961,
President John Kennedy
made him a judge
on a U.S. Court of Appeals.

Thurgood Marshall (above) appeared before Senate committees.
The senators talked for nearly a year before agreeing to Marshall's
appointment. Marshall (below) was the first African American
ever appointed to the U.S. Court of Appeals.

But the Senate had to
say yes to this.
It took them almost a year.
Some senators didn't
want a black judge.

Then, on July 13, 1965,
President Lyndon Johnson
asked Thurgood to be
solicitor general for the
United States.

Thurgood Marshall is sworn in as solicitor general of the United States as President Lyndon Johnson and Marshall's family look on.

Again the Senate must say yes.
This time it took them
less than one month.

As solicitor general, Thurgood was the lawyer for the government in Supreme Court cases. He argued 19 cases in all and won 14 of them.

Then an even more important job came along.

Thurgood Marshall and three of his aides meet in his Department of Justice office. As solicitor general, Marshall was interested in the "problems of humanity."

Chapter 5

Justice Thurgood Marshall

On June 13, 1967,
President Lyndon Johnson
asked Thurgood to be a
justice on the Supreme Court.
He said yes and
so did the Senate.

Opposite page: President Lyndon Johnson asked
Marshall to serve on the Supreme Court.

Thurgood was
the first
African American
to serve on the
Supreme Court.
He must have
thought about
all those other
fighters in
his family.

How proud
they would be!

**The Supreme Court in 1967. Chief Justice
Earl Warren is in the front row, center.**

As he took his place on the Supreme Court, Marshall
swore "to do equal right to the poor and the rich."

At first he worked
quietly on the court.
Some people didn't think
he was a fighter at all.

Then Thurgood began
to speak up.

He felt it was wrong to
punish people for a crime
by killing them
—and he said so.

Thurgood Marshall in 1977

Marshall gets a last-minute checkup from his wife before taking the oath as Supreme Court justice.

He felt that police must obey the laws when they go after criminals—and he said so.

Most of all, he felt that all people must be treated equally. Thurgood said that again and again.

The Supreme Court in early 1991. Top row (from left) Anthony Kennedy, Sandra Day O'Connor, Antonin Scalia, David Souter. Front row: Harry Blackmun, Byron White, Chief Justice William Rehnquist, Thurgood Marshall, John Paul Stevens.

Thurgood Marshall was
in his 80's when he
left the Supreme Court.
He was still full of fight.

He hoped that when
people talked about
him they would say,
"He did what he could
with what he had."

Important Dates

1908	July 2—Born in Baltimore, Maryland, to Norma and William Marshall
1928	Married Vivien Burey
1933	Graduated from Howard University Law School Became lawyer for Baltimore chapter of NAACP
1936	Began work at NAACP headquarters in New York City
1954	Won *Brown v. Board of Education of Topeka*
1955	Married Cecilia Suyat
1961	Named judge to United States Court of Appeals for the Second Circuit
1965	Named solicitor general of the United States
1967-1991	Served as justice on the Supreme Court
1993	January 24—Died of heart failure in Bethesda, Maryland

INDEX

Page numbers in boldface type indicate illustrations.

PHOTO CREDITS

ABOUT THE AUTHOR

Carol Greene has degrees in English literature and musicology. She has worked in international exchange programs, as an editor, and as a teacher of writing. She now lives in Webster Groves, Missouri, and writes full-time. She has published more than 100 books, including those in the Rookie Biographies series.